First Facts™

Everyday Character Education

Peacefulness

by Rebecca Olien

Consultant:
Madonna Murphy, PhD, Professor of Education
University of St. Francis, Joliet, Illinois
Author, *Character Education in America's Blue Ribbon Schools*

Capstone
press
Mankato, Minnesota

First Facts is published by Capstone Press,
151 Good Counsel Drive, P.O. Box 669, Mankato, Minnesota 56002.
www.capstonepress.com

Library of Congress Cataloging-in-Publication Data
Olien, Rebecca
    Peacefulness / Rebecca Olien.
    p. cm.—(First facts. Everyday character education)
    Summary: "Introduces peacefulness through examples of everyday situations where this
character trait can be used"—Provided by publisher.
    Includes bibliographical references and index.
    ISBN 0-7368-4280-2 (hardcover)
    1. Conduct of life—Juvenile literature. 2. Conflict Management—Juvenile literature
3. Interpersonal Conflict—Juvenile literature I. Title. II. Series.
BJ1595.O45 2006
179'.7—dc22
                             2004026765

Editorial Credits
Becky Viaene, editor; Molly Nei, set designer; Kate Opseth, book designer;
    Wanda Winch, photo researcher/photo editor

Photo Credits
Capstone Press/Karon Dubke, cover, 1, 5, 6–7, 8, 9, 10–11, 12, 13, 19, 21
Digital Vision Ltd./Tony Sweet, 1 (background)
Kidz Voice LA/Constantina Milonopoulos, 14–15
Library of Congress, 17
©The Nobel Foundation, 20

1 2 3 4 5 6 10 09 08 07 06 05

Table of Contents

Peacefulness

Miranda and her brother Tom want to watch different TV shows. Miranda turns on her show. Tom tries to take the remote away from Miranda.

Miranda stays **calm**. She and Tom talk peacefully. They agree to take turns using the TV. Miranda gives Tom the remote so he can take his turn.

Fact!
Peacefulness means being calm and happy with yourself. Peaceful people solve problems without using violence.

At Your School

Being peaceful helps make school a better place. The student council meets and talks about how to improve the school. Each person has an **opinion** about how to do things. You disagree with some students, but you listen to their ideas peacefully.

! Fact!
Coming up with solutions to problems is a way to promote peacefulness.

With Your Friends

Friends get along better when they are peaceful. You and a friend want to play different games. You talk about the games.

Talking and listening help you get along with friends peacefully. You **compromise** and play a different game.

At Home

At supper, your family members take turns talking about their day. You may feel bad about something that happened at school.

Talking about problems can help. Your family helps you think of ways to solve a problem. Sharing your feelings is a healthy way to feel peaceful.

In Your Community

People work together to make their **community** a peaceful place. You are at an arcade. You see two kids arguing over who will use a game next.

You suggest that instead of arguing, they both play. Thinking up peaceful solutions helps solve problems safely.

Milonopoulos Twins

Kids can make their city a better place. Niko and Theo Milonopoulos work for peace in Los Angeles. The twin brothers were upset by shootings in their community. They gathered more than 7,000 kids' signatures to **ban** selling bullets in Los Angeles.

Fact!
In 2000, Niko and Theo won the President's Service Award.

14

Jane Addams

Jane Addams believed nations should work together for peace. She was against World War I (1914–1918). She gave many speeches about peace. Addams was head of the Women's Peace Party. In 1931, she received the Nobel Peace Prize for her work.

Fact!
Jane Addams was also president of the Women's International League for Peace and Freedom.

Jane Addams

What Would You Do?

Liz and Emily are at Miranda's house. Liz doesn't want to make a scrapbook with Miranda and Emily. Liz is upset. She wants to make bracelets. What could Miranda do to find a peaceful solution?

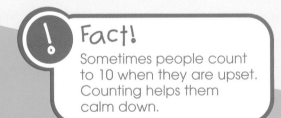

Fact!
Sometimes people count to 10 when they are upset. Counting helps them calm down.

Amazing but True!

The Nobel Peace Prize was started by the inventor of **dynamite**. Alfred Nobel made a lot of money selling dynamite to countries at war. At the end of his life, Nobel understood the importance of peace. He gave his money away to award people who work for peace.

Hands On: Peace T-shirt

What words and symbols show peacefulness?
Try this activity to see how you can show peacefulness.

What You Need

newspapers

puffy paint

T-shirt

What You Do

1. Look in newspapers for articles
   and pictures showing people working together peacefully.
2. Use puffy paint on the T-shirt to write words and draw
   pictures of peaceful examples you find in newspapers.
3. Continue to add words and pictures showing peace until
   the T-shirt is full. Let the T-shirt dry for one day.
4. Seeing and talking about ways to act peacefully can help
   people want to do more. Wear your T-shirt to show others
   examples of peace.

   What are some ways to act peacefully? How can acting in
a peaceful way help the world be less violent?

Glossary

ban (BAN)—to not allow

calm (KAHM)—quiet and peaceful

community (kuh-MYOO-nuh-tee)—a group of people who live in the same area

compromise (KOM-pruh-mize)—an agreement where all sides agree to something different from what they want

dynamite (DYE-nuh-mite)—a powerful explosive used to blow up things

opinion (uh-PIN-yuhn)—a person's ideas and beliefs about something

Read More

Raatma, Lucia. *Peacefulness.* Character Education. Mankato, Minn.: Bridgestone Books, 2000.

Radunsky, Vladimir. *What Does Peace Feel Like?* New York: Atheneum Books for Young Readers, 2004.

Internet Sites

FactHound offers a safe, fun way to find Internet sites related to this book. All of the sites on FactHound have been researched by our staff.

Here's how:
1. Visit *www.facthound.com*
2. Type in this special code **0736842802** for age-appropriate sites. Or enter a search word related to this book for a more general search.
3. Click on the **Fetch It** button.

FactHound will fetch the best sites for you!

Index